99 Journal Writing Templates

To Get You Writing Today

By: Norman T. Bell

Text Copyright © 2013
REZZnet
All Rights Reserved

No right to redistribute, copy, amend or exploit materials. The information presented represents the view of the author at the date of publication and not the publisher, and by rate at which conditions change, the author reserves rights to update opinions based on new conditions. Neither author nor publisher assume any responsibility for errors or omissions. This book is in no way endorsed or distributed by any brand/company/site/etc. listed herin, are the sole opinions of the author, and should be treated as such.

Preface To 99 Journal Writing Templates:

First of all, congratulations for taking interest in journal writing. Writing in a journal is one of the most intimate and mind-enhancing activities you can do.

You can learn a lot from journaling - and not just about yourself, but about the world, and how you view it. Just by simply writing down your thoughts, you can gain loads of insight that you previously didn't have. Journaling also allows you to look back on how you may have viewed things in the past - you can then see how you've changed, how you've progressed.

There's so many benefits of journal writing, it's just one of those activities and experiences where you get to be by yourself, with no other worries in the world. Just you, a pencil, and your journal. You can journal by yourself or with friends. You can journal in a journal, a notebook, a diary, a white sheet of paper, heck even on post it notes! As long as you are writing, that's all that matters. One quick tip - write down the dates on each entry! It's more fun to look back on what you wrote down on an exact day rather than guessing.

99 Journal Writing Templates gives you just that. In this book, you'll lead yourself through 99 different templates and prompts for writing in your journal.

Whether or not you feel stuck when writing in your journal, this list of 99 templates will get you on the right track, and give you content ideas you can use for MONTHS.

Hope you like the book, and enjoy the journal writing templates!

1 - Quote

What It Means To You

Write down a quote, then write down what it means to you.

It can be a quote that you made up yourself, or a quote from someone else. It can be from memory, or from research you do right now.

From time to time, or whenever you find a new favorite quote - write it down in your journal. You can learn a lot from quotes, especially positive, inspiring thoughts and messages. What's even more important is what YOU think and feel about the quote.

2

Sentence From A Book

Take a sentence from a book, and write about it.

You have GOT to have a book, right? If not, that's okay. You can go to Amazon.com, search for a book, and then click "look inside", and you'll have tons of content to work with.

This can be a sentence or statement that is powerful, interesting to you, weird or shocking. As long as it's directly from a book, you are good to go. Write about what you think of the statement/sentence, and how you feel it could be expanded upon.

3

Embarrassing Moment

Write about an embarrassing moment from your past.

You can write the first thing that comes to mind, but what's even better is if you actually think back, WAY back, and try to think of a truly embarrassing moment in your life.

Most people have embarrassing moments that they've forgotten about all together. Although it was embarrassing back in the day, you'll find that looking back on these embarrassing moments and memories allows you to smile, laugh, and think about your past experiences.

Embarrassing moments shouldn't be experiences that you regret - they should be things you can write about, think about, and learn from.

4

Recent Film

Write about a movie you recently watched, like your own movie review.

Have you ever wanted to be a film critic? It's one of the most fun jobs in the world! Imagine being able to watch movies for a living, and then say how good or bad they are.

Well, this is your chance, right here, right now. Pick a movie you recently watched. If you haven't watched any movies recently, pick a movie that you've seen in the past, maybe a favorite movie.

Write about the characters, the plot, and twists and turns in the movie. Write about what you liked, what you didn't like, you can even write about how the movie SHOULD have ended!

5

Experiences - Being Scared

Write about things that scare you/scary experiences.

We've all had scary and frightening experiences in our lives. I'm sure you can think of more than one instance in which you were scared, frightened, shocked, nervous.

Writing about scary experiences allows you to tell the world that you know it happened, you know it exists, and you are okay with it, because it is over.

Think of this like getting rid of your fears. Laugh about this experience, write down why it was scary, how it was funny (if at all), and what you learned from it or now do differently.

6

Dreams and Nightmares

Write about your dreams and nightmares.

100% of people dream every single night (that is, the people who actually go to sleep!).

It's true, even if you don't remember your dreams, you are still dreaming when you are asleep.

I used to hate when I would remember a dream when I woke up, but then forget about the entire dream minutes later. So, what I did was start to write down my dreams and nightmares right when I wake up.

You can learn a LOT from your dreams. You can dissect and uncover real and true meanings of dreams, and you can even later look up and research what your dream meant.

7

What I've Learned...

Write down things that you've learned in life.

People learn new things every day - and so do you.

In this journal post, write down one (or more) thing(s) you've learned in your life. Think of this as you own little tip book/section that you can look back on later.

When you write down things you've learned in life, you are able to avoid making the same mistakes again, as well as keep the good lessons you've learned handy for future viewing and/or sharing.

8

Letter Starts

Write as many words as you can that start with a specific letter.

This is a fun one.

There's no true meaning behind this type of journal post, this is just for fun, and to see how many words you can name that start with a specific letter.

For instance - apple, apostrophe, apparatus, apparel, angel, angle, a-hole, answer, application, at, align - you get the idea.

This is a fun little exercise you can do time and time again - in fact you can do this 26 times (over time) for all the letters in the alphabet!

9

The Bucket List

Write down your full or condensed bucket list.

Ahh... the good ol' bucket list.

A bucket list is simply a list of things you want to do before you die. The term is said to be originated in many different places - we'll never really know exactly where it came from.

However, what it really use to mean was when someone didn't want to do something today, they'd "throw it in the bucket", meaning they'll *get to it later.*

So, what do you want to do before you die? Really think about it... If you could do anything in the world, what would you do? This exercise is fun to do every few months to see if your mind has changed, as well as seeing if you actually did anything on your bucket list from last time!

10

Improving Talents

Write about your talents and how you can improve on them.

We all have talents. And better yet, we all have DIFFERENT talents. You are probably a lot different than I, and frankly, that's awesome.

What talents do you have? Write them down. Then, after writing down the talents you have right now, think about and write down what you need to do in order to improve on them.

This exercise and journal entry allows you to set goals for yourself, and keep yourself moving forward. When you write down what you need to do to improve your own talents, you are giving yourself the first step to actually improving on them. Thoughts lead to feelings which lead to actions, which lead to RESULTS. Find out how to get those results in this entry.

11

How Was Your Day?

How was your day? Go ahead, write about it.

Self explanatory much? This exercise is easy, and is one of the most common exercises and journal entries among writers.

How was your day, what did you do, what didn't you do, what did you want to do? How did you feel? Anything fun or interesting happen?

The "how was your day" journal entry is nice, because it allows you to look back on specific dates, and what happened on specific days of the year. Check it out, a year from now you can look back to this very day and see what you wrote, and compare it to your "1 year from now" journal entry.

12

What Bothers Me?

Write about things that bother you.

It's okay if you have things that are bothersome in your life. However, it's NOT okay to keep it inside forever.

One of the easiest ways to get the negative energy off your chest is by getting it on paper. Write a journal entry about things or people who bother you. Think about the root cause of the bothersome feelings, and try to connect with these feelings on a deeper level.

When you write down what bothers you, you are able to get a complete sense and look at what it is you need to stay away from, avoid, change, etc.

13

The Gratitude Post

Write down little things that you like and/or notice about people.

Show gratitude for your loved ones by writing a post showing your gratitude. Write whatever comes to your mind when you think about this person(s).

Whether it's a family member, parent, sibling, friend, partner, spouse - showing gratitude on paper allows you to feel good thoughts about the important people in your life.

You know as well as I do that life can get tough, and sometimes the people closest to us can hurt us. However, don't let that stop you from remembering the good things about your loved ones. Keep this page positive energy only.

14

Else Description

Write a journal entry as if someone else was describing you.

This goes way further than you describing someone else, as well as someone else describing you. This entry digs deep in your mind, and can show you how you think other people (or another person in general) perceive(s) you.

You might be surprised when you start to think about the different situations and experiences you and this other person have been in together. Through it all, how would this person describe you?

You can go with visual and physical descriptions, you can also go with mental and psychological descriptions. Would your friend describe you as fun, pushy, beautiful, amazing? It's okay if some are good and some are bad, the point is to think outside your own head, and connect with others on a subconscious level.

15

Sketch n' Draw

In this journal entry, all you have to do is SKETCH and DRAW.

I love art, any kind. Painting, drawing, sculpting - it's all fun for me.

Whether or not you like to sketch or draw, and whether or not you are good at it, just do it - art is therapeutic.

You don't have to be the next Picasso or Michelangelo, in fact it is better if you aren't. Sketch all over a full page in your journal, and just have fun. Draw shapes, cartoons, random scribbles. Draw your pet, your family, or just anything random.

The point is to just get the pencil or pen on paper. You shouldn't be focused on getting it to "look right", because in my mind, ALL art looks right. Do this same "sketch n' draw" journal entry every once in awhile, and after you've done it a few times, look back on your old drawings.

Not only will you be able to see how you've improved, but you will also be able to see what sorts of things you sketched before, and how the imagery of your drawings change over time (which can then open up even more personal journal entries).

16

Hidden Codes

Write a journal entry with hidden messages encoded.

Here, easy languages lack origin.

***That line/sentence right above is encoded. Can you figure out what the hidden message is? Take a look at the first letter of every word. H - e - l - l - o. Cool, right? And that's just something extremely basic.

Try to think of your own code you can come up with, and encode hidden and secret messages into some of journal entries.

The fun part is looking back on it, reading it regular, thinking you may have been crazy at that time in your life, and then realize you encoded a message for yourself to read 10 years later! A lot can be done with this - If you are stuck, just use the example I gave.

17

Language Developing

Develop your own language, word by word.

This isn't meant to create a whole new language entirely, I'm not asking you to rewrite the dictionary here.

What I'm saying is, start with some easy words. Simple things you say each day like "Hi" and "How are you?" and "Good morning, good night", things like that. Then, every once in awhile, create new words and translations.

For "Hi", it could be "Laha", then for "Hello" it could be "Loohoo". 'Good morning' turns into 'Raag gooring".

Yes, I just thought of these, and you can too, right now. Write down simple translations at first, then later on you can start to write full sentences in your own language.

If your mind gets boggled - that's good! This type of activity entertains and works your brain, and is actually said to raise your IQ. But most of all, it's fun, especially if you teach your language to 1 other person. Everyone will think you are from some foreign land - everyone.

18

Letter To Thy Self

Write a letter to yourself to look back on in the future.

Start with...

Dear [Your Name],

Then, write a letter to yourself right now. Tell yourself what you are thinking, what you think you will be doing a year from now, 5 years from now, even 10 years from now.

What do you do on the weekends? I'm sure it will change over time, and it's fun to look back on what you used to do, especially because most people grow and change every year.

19

Date Recorder

Record important dates in your life.

The reason most people stop writing in their journal is because most of the time, there's not a whole lot to write in a journal every day.

Too many people focus on just writing about their day, and when it gets boring for a few days, and a habit is started of not writing, journaling becomes non-existant pretty fast.

Now, that's exactly why I wrote this book of journal writing templates - to give you fun entries, templates, and exercises to use whenever you want.

And for this journal entry, instead of writing your daily life every single day, only take record of the BIG events and fun days you had.

It's always better to look back on good memories, and you'll never stop journaling, because whenever a fun event happens, you know you are going to want to write it down so you can look back on the awesome memories years from now.

20

Short Story Time

Write a short story, any length you want.

This one is easy. If you get stuck, start with "Once upon a time...", that always does the trick.

Your short story can be fiction, non-fiction, short, long, whatever you want. As long as you are telling some sort of a story, that's all that matters.

Writing short stories (and creative writing in general) makes you smarter and more creative, there's no doubt about it.

21

Best Experiences

Write about your best experiences from the past.

You should now be recording your fun experiences when they happen (or that night), but I'm sure you haven't been journaling since you were a baby.

Take a minute or two to think back on the absolute best experiences you've had in your lifetime. Don't be worried if you can't think of any off the top of your head - you'll think of some.

As I've said before, writing about GOOD experiences allows you to look back in your journal years from now and smile and laugh.

Think about time with friends and family, maybe a vacation you took, or how about funny school experiences? For now, just think of one, and write about it. When you think of others, you can make it your next journal entry.

22

New Words, Vocab!

Write new words that you learn.

Yeah yeah, no one likes vocab. But I honestly wish I paid more attention in high school during vocabulary lessons.

It's been proven, when you learn more new words, you get smarter. And when you do it daily, you get smarter every day. Same goes with reading and writing, which you are already doing, so you're ahead of the pack!

If you learn a new word, write it down in your journal. Look it up, write down what it means. By doing this, you increase your vocab skills as well as your writing skills - not to mention the more proper conversations you will start to have.

Above all, it's fun to learn new words. If you haven't learned a new word in awhile, or can't remember one right now, do a search online or flip to a random page in the dictionary. There are words all over the place.

23

Any Word

Write about any word that comes to your mind.

Think of any word. Got it? Now write it down!

Then, write about it.

I thought of "apples" for some reason. So... mine would go like this:

Apples, they are red, they are a fruit, I remember the book Johnny Appleseed, the song apples and bananas, apples actually can be any color, not just red, but green too.

See? It doesn't have to be anything perfect, just get words on the paper. Writing descriptions of things makes connections in your brain between different words, different mind flashes in your brain, could even bring up memories. Notice how I brought up Johnny Appleseed. I remember that book, and now I'm starting to remember the first time I read it. Good times =)

24

Confrontation

Prepare for confrontation.

This journal entry obviously works better if you know confrontation is coming, but it's also valuable even if you don't think it's coming. At least you'll be prepared.

Just think of ANY thing that someone could confront you about, and write down what your response would be.

If your spouse, child, or other family member has a problem with you about something, figure out the best way to respond. Sometimes, I've written down what I would say, and realized it would be the WORST thing to talk about first. This allows us to get out how we feel right away, and then think about it before actually being confronted.

You don't need an answer for everything, but you can learn a lot from what you write down in this entry. This makes you able to handle any situation that may arise.

25

Hopes And Prayers

Write your hopes and prayers for yourself and/or others.

Whether or not you believe in God or any type of god, you can still pray to SOMEONE.

I in fact pray to specific people. I feel that when I put my positive hopes, prayers, and energy out in the word specifically for single person, that it may do more than just simply praying.

It's nice to think it, better to say it out loud, and best to write it down. Who are you praying for today? Is someone sick, in the hospital? Are you hoping that your boyfriend proposes? Are you praying for someone who is sad or depressed?

Whatever your hopes and prayers are for today, write them down: "I pray for my nephew Wilson, he cut his knee against a nail yesterday, and I hope he gets better." There, it's that easy.

26

Lists Of Wants And Needs

Create lists of things you need or want to do.

This journal entry can be written in a few different ways.

You can of course just start listing all of things you want to do, as well as all of the things you need to get done or need to do today/this week.

Another great way to do this exercise is first writing down everything you WANT, and THEN writing down everything you need.

You'll start to notice some similarities, but probably a lot of differences. This allows you establish what's really necessary in your life, and what you should focus on.

27

What Did You Eat?

Write about what you ate today.

What did you eat today? If you write in your journal first thing in the morning, what did you eat last night or yesterday?

If you don't eat very well, or usually have the same things every day, write about your favorite meal, your favorite restaurant, your favorite dish!

WARNING: This may make you hungry, so have a snack while you write this journal entry!

It's fun to look back and see what you were eating "back in the day", and how your taste buds and mind changes on the food you eat over time.

28

Rich Ideas

Write about your own get rich ideas and thoughts.

Most people call them "get rich quick schemes". However, I'm not telling you to write a scheme OR a scam!

Most rich people started from nothing, and their fortunes started with one thing - AN IDEA.

So, start getting those ideas on paper! First, write what you are interested in doing in life. Write about what you dream of doing. Figure out if there is a market for it, how you can make a lot of money with it, and what you have to do now to get it started.

You never know, you may just be the next multi-billionaire.

29

Poetry And Rhymes

Write poetry, rhymes, and/or raps.

Sitting here writing, while all my family's fighting,

Want to get away, but I have to stay.

The little butterfly flies high in the sky,

It flies so high, oh me, oh my!

It doesn't have to be anything grammy-worthy. Just write down some rhymes, some poetry - or even a rap!

This journal entry should be fun. You can even write about your day in a page-full of rhymes and raps.

30

Song Parody

Write down your own parody of any song.

You've seen it on YouTube, you've seen them on TV. Ever hear of "Weird Al"?

Take your favorite song, and change up the lyrics! You can change up just one or two words in the chorus, or you can make it an entirely different song!

Once you have your song written, try singing it - maybe even shoot a video and post it online.

10 years from now, when you dig your journal out of your old never-touched box of things, you'll laugh at the song, and may not even know what song it is!

31

Life Goals

Write about goals you have in and for your life.

Everyone has goals, no matter how big or small. Your goals might be to rule the world, or it may be just to get through the day.

No matter how big or small your goals are, get writing. When you write about your goals, you are telling the world that THIS is what you want. Ever heard of "The Secret"? Well although it doesn't work for most people, you will find that the more you talk about and write about your goals, the more likely they are to happen.

Also, when you write your goals now and look back on them later, you can see what you've accomplished, and what you haven't.

32

Feeling

How do you FEEL? Write down specific emotions.

It's emotional journal time!

You don't need to go overboard, but write down how you feel. How do you feel RIGHT NOW? How did you feel yesterday?

Sad, happy, excited, worried, stressed, amazing, awesome - but don't just write down adjectives, write down WHY you feel this way. Act like your own psychiatrist.

33

5 Senses

Write using all 5 of your senses - taste, smell, touch, hearing, sight.

The easiest way to start this entry is to write down the 5 senses like this...

- TASTE: - HEAR:

- SMELL: - SIGHT:

- TOUCH:

Then, write down the different things you sense. What flavors were left on your toungue and in your mouth from earlier? Do you smell anything - if you can't smell anything fragrant, how would you describe the "nothingness" smell?

How do the pages of your journal feel in your hand? Do you hear anything close to you, or maybe further away? What do you see?

Whenever you are using one of your senses, it's best to try to block out your others as best you can. For instance, when you are focusing on smell, close your eyes and cover your ears.

This will increase your senses, and shows you how you describe certain things that are actually sometimes very hard to describe.

34

Today's History

Write about today's historical events.

EVERY DAY is history.

What I mean is, every single day out of the 365 each year has historical significance. Every single one. Do some 1 minute research about today. You'll find hundreds of different things that happened in history.

So, what happened today that was so special years ago?

Find something that has the most significance to you, and write about it. I hope this shows you that every day is indeed special, and ANYTHING can happen on any day of the year.

35

Hobby Writing

Do you have any hobbies? Write about them here.

Of course one of your hobbies is journal writing, right?!

But besides writing, what other hobbies do you have? In fact, if you don't have any other hobbies, write about writing! What makes writing special for you?

Everyone has at least one hobby. Write about what the hobby means to you, how you got started with it, who else you know has the same hobby, and anything else about your hobby that makes it worthwhile.

You can even do research on where your specific hobby originated, or who the leaders in your hobbyist industry are.

36

Tasks

Write about your tasks, whether it's homework, job related, etc.

This isn't just about what you have to do VS what you want to do, it's more than that.

This is like your to-do list. If you are in school, what homework do you have to do? Got a job? - Write about the tasks you must do at work.

And besides work and/or school, what other things do you have to do today, this week, this month?

First, write them down in a list format. Then, write down what you MUST get done first, second... last - you get the idea. The first step to action is vocalizing/writing it down. Write down the tasks you want and need to do, and you'll be more likely to get them done in a timely manner.

37

Travel And Places

Write about places you want to travel to.

I for one like to travel the world. Anywhere and everywhere is my travel destination.

But for most people, you probably have that one place you want to visit, or visit again!

Write down where you want to travel to, and why. What makes this place so special? Is it the weather, the scenery, the new people - just getting away?

38

Compare And Contrast

Compare and contrast 2 different things, it can be anything.

Start with 'something'. It can be yourself, it can be another person, it can be someone famous, even a sport, or a physical item - ANYTHING.

When you write your first thing down, now think of something that is in the same category, and compare and contrast it. Compare 2 people, 2 sports, 2 items, etc.

After you do that, compare and contrast 2 completely different things! Compare yourself to an ice cream cone, compare your bicycle to baseball!

It's easy to compare and contrast two similar items or things in the same category, but it's more difficult (and more fun) to compare and contrast two completely different things. Try it!

39

Controversy

Write about controversial topics in this journal entry.

Ever had to deal with controversy?

Controversial topics aren't for the dinner table, and they aren't for parties. They aren't for friends, and they aren't for people who think differently than you. SO WHAT IS CONTROVERSY GOOD FOR?

Controversy is perfect for a nice, long... journal entry!

That's right, start with any controversial topic - but specifically one that you can connect with. Write about what it means to you, and why you believe it is so controversial. If you don't think it should be controversial, say why!

40

Extra, Extra!

Write a catchy newspaper headline and write your own story.

Extra Extra, Read all about it! This journal entry has now turned into your own newspaper story.

Start with a headline, it can be anything - even about yourself! "Man/Woman Fights Off 10 Burglars Without A Scratch!". Make sure it's JUICY.

Once you've written your juicy headline, write your story as if you were a newspaper writer or someone reporting on it.

41

Fictional Letter

Write a fictional letter or postcard to someone.

Start with your fictional person. Who is this person, and why are you writing to them?

Once you have the person you are writing to in mind, go ahead and write a letter to them. Tell them about your day, tell them about life in general.

Ask how they are doing, and what they've been up to. It doesn't matter that they aren't going to respond, at least you can get it on paper.

This is mainly just to get you in the habit of writing, but also gives you more practice with communication through writing. Sometimes people perceive things differently when they can't communicate face to face, so this allows you to show how you truly feel, through writing.

42

Advertisement

Make and create your own advertisement, draw it right in your journal.

The average person sees hundreds of ads each day, and will most likely see millions in their lifetime.

An ad doesn't have to be a commercial or a pre-roll video or even a direct ad in a newspaper. Advertising has been around for a very long time, even before it was called advertising. Before, it was called "persuasion".

So for this journal entry, choose something to advertise. It can be a product, a lifestyle, an event, even a person. Then, draw or write some juicy ad copy that will persuade them to do what you want.

The more ads you draw and write, and the more you work on your copy, the more people will be willing to do what you say. It's just the art of persuasion - Don't use this for evil!

43

And Then What Happened?

Write a story where every line starts with "and then".

If you have kids, do you notice their stories usually have the word "and then" plastered all over them?

Even if you don't have kids, you remember when you were a kid, right?

"I did this, and then I went here, and then Cindy said this, and then Brian got mad, and then we left, and then we came back, and then the teacher came, and then we got in trouble."

Well, that's what this journal entry is all about - "And Then."

Start with one line. "I went to the movies" or something like that. Once that is written, make every single line start with "And then". Fill up your entire page, and read back your story. You may feel out of breath after, since you just wrote one of the longest run-on sentences ever. But, it's surely fun, and supplies your journal with a funny story.

44

Thankful

Write down what you are thankful for.

This is something my family always does at Thanksgiving. But of course, not everyone celebrates Thanksgiving (or you do, but don't believe in all the religious stuff).

No matter who you are, it's good to be thankful. It's sad to say that I've been beaten, pushed around, lied to all my life - but I'm still thankful for lots of things. I just had to think about it a little while longer than most other people.

Are you thankful for the clothes on your back? How about the shoes that half the world doesn't own? If you can't think of anything, write down why you are thankful to be living.

This gives your journal, your present self, AND your future self more happiness, more thankfulness, and shows you that you do have it better than at least some people out there, probably most.

45

Wish List

If you could make a wish list, what would be on it?

Okay, this one is one of those quirky fun journal entries. Around Christmastime/holidays, my neices, nephews, young cousins - they would all write the items they wanted for Christmas on a "Wish List".

But away from Christmas, wish lists are everywhere. Amazon, facebook, apps, websites, and lots of other places I'm sure. A wish list is essentially a list you make of all the things you WISH you had or could have.

Do you want new shoes, maybe a computer? What accessories come with the computer? In this journal entry, you can go crazy. Write down all the different things you want in life and wish you could have.

Then, if you want to take it a step further, find out the TOTAL PRICE of your entire wish list put together. Don't worry, this number will be huge. Mine was in the millions. I may not be able to buy everything or have everything on my list, but at least I put it out there in the world (and in fact, I've actually been able to cross some things off).

46

Mapping Success

Write a map, a map that maps your way to success.

This can be a map like a treasure map, or like a map of the real world. It can also be little islands or circles that link to eachother.

No matter what map you make, it's important that you not only draw out the successes, but also the failures and obstacles that may come along the way.

This journal entry allows you to lay out a path for yourself. Success is different for everyone. For some it's money, for others it's being happy, for others it all comes down to freedom.

Just start writing and drawing a map that shows your path to success, whatever that success may be for you.

47

What if...?

Ask yourself, "what if this happened?", and write about it.

What if the world ran out of food? What if the sun stopped shining? What if fish could fly?

This can be a fun entry, or even a detailed "what if the world ended" entry. Either way, you should pick at least one question starting with "what if", and then write a detailed response to the question.

48

Collaborative Writing

When you have a friend or family member with you, write a collaborative journal entry.

This is the only 2-person journal entry exercise and template. I believe that journal writing is a one-person thing, but I did want to include this in case you are one who likes to journal with friends or groups.

When writing collaboratively in a journal, it's easiest to start with a fictional story. You can go back and forth and continue writing one story, and then have some one read it aloud once it's finished.

Another way you could do this entry is with real life stuff. Whatever you or your friend/sibling/partner want to write, go for it! If someone doesn't feel like writing anything, they can draw something instead. There's no limits with fun collaborative journal writing.

49

Scribble Time

Scribble all over the page. You'll love it.

You may not think this to be worthwhile, but scribbling random swirls and zig zags and chicken-scratch can really relieve your stress.

I used to do it when I was a kid - in fact it was a tip from one of my teachers. I would continue to tap my foot on the tile floor, and it would bug the heck out of everyone around me. So, I started to scribble when I was anxious or stressed, and it helped out - not just me, but the people around me.

Unless you are low on pen ink or pencil graphite, I would say fill up this whole page! Keep drawing and scribbling and writing until every inch is covered.

NOTE: You may want to put a magazine or something underneath the page you scribble on, otherwise you could rip through the paper, or worse, rip through 10 pages!

50

How To

Write about how to do something, step by step.

Everyone knows how to do something step by step. Whether it's putting together an engine of a car, making a ham sandwich, or tying shoes, everyone knows how to do something.

So, in this journal entry, write down the step by step instructions on how to do something. Make your instructions so easy that ANYONE can follow them and get the same results.

51

Comic Strip

Make your own comic strip, right here, right now.

Forget about drawing in general or just scribbling in your journal - it's time to draw and write your own comic strip!

This comic can be 1 square (using the whole page), 4 squares, or even have 20 or more squares and fill up multiple pages. It can also be in any style, and doesn't have to look like a normal comic strip.

Your comic can be funny or not, black and white or full color. It can tell jokes, or it can describe your day, or both!

Mindmap Creation

Create a mindmap for anything you want.

I love mindmaps. This sort of works like the "mapping your way to success" journal entry, but instead of a one-road map, you are instead starting in the middle, and branching out from all sides.

Start with a circle in the middle of the page. Now write your main topic or 'thing' in this circle. Then, draw lines that go off of your circle in all directions, and create/connect them to more circles. In these circles, you will write a type of 'sub-topic'. You can keep branching off until you get super-detailed.

It's hard to explain without an example, so let me give you an example - I'll use THIS BOOK.

In my middle circle, I would start with "99 Journal Writing Templates". Then I could branch it off into 11 sections, like "fun templates", "serious templates", "language arts templates", "long templates", "short templates", etc.

After that, I could break those 11 into 9 more each (99 total in this branch), and each circle would be a chapter title. And if I wanted, I could branch them out even further, and include a lot more detail.

You get the picture. And these mindmaps work for anything. "Food" can break into 100s (1 being fruit), and fruit can break into hundreds (1 being apples), then apples can break into the different types of apples - and 1 specific apple can be broken down into facts about that one type of apple. Just get started with mindmaps - they'll open up your mind.

53

Learning From Mistakes

Write about how you learned from a mistake in the past.

Everyone makes mistakes. I have, you have, my parents have, your parents have.

However, although everyone makes mistakes, NOT everyone learns from their mistakes. This journal entry will let you learn from your mistakes.

Pick any mistake you've made in life. This can be a small mistake from today or yesterday, or it can be a big mistake from years ago.

Once you write down the mistake you made, now write about how you learned from your mistake. What made you make this mistake in the first place? How could you have handled it differently? Have you made the mistake multiple times? Why?

Not only will you learn from your mistake, but you'll also show yourself that you have the power to not make the same mistake again.

54

Biography

Write a short biography about someone else.

This biography should be short. It can also be about anyone you choose, not just celebrities or famous people in history.

The first step is choosing someone to write a biography about. Choose your mom, dad, brother or sister, one of your friends, someone you know, your favorite music artist, someone you look up to.

Now write about them. Start with your own knowledge about the person. Then, if you need to, do some research on the person (if they are more well-known), and you'll find out even more cool facts that you may not have known before.

55

Autobiography

Write a short autobiography about yourself.

So you've already written about someone else, now it's time to write about yourself!

Have you ever read someone's autobiography before? Most of the time, they sound like one of the most amazing people in the world. And although I'm not saying any particular person isn't amazing, all I'm saying is some facts may not really be facts.

You don't have to worry if your mini-journal-autobiography has one or two made up facts. In fact, you can make up the entire thing if you want. Write an autobiography about how you wish or want to sound/be.

56

Script Writing

Write a script for a play, a show, a movie, etc.

Script writing is fun! This doesn't have to turn into any type of masterpiece, as long as you have a general story line or character reference, or even just a quick summary or plot.

What's your fancy? Play, show, movie? Whatever you want to write for, start with a setting, a background, a place. Then, who's your main character? You can write about some of the supporting characters and roles they play, as well as what your story is about.

You never know - your little script scribbles could turn into a book, and later a movie, or play, or a show!

57

Interview Questions

Write interview questions for someone famous or fictional.

These questions should be for someone either famous or fictional. If they are indeed fictional (fake/made-up), then make it as if this person is important, like the president of something, or the CEO of a company, or someone who has accomplished a lot in their life.

What would you ask this person? Does this person have the knowledge that can change the world, feed the world, free the world? Not only should you be writing initial questions, but you should also think about how they would respond, and what follow-up questions you would have for them.

This journal entry gets you asking questions, and gets you searching for the truth. There is so much you and I don't know about people, the world, life. Keep asking questions, and keep writing them in your journal!

58

Funny Jokes

Got any funny jokes? Write them in a journal entry!

First, even if you can't think of a joke off the top of your head, go search for one. Find a funny one, and write the joke in a journal entry.

Once you have at least one joke in your journal, then when you think of and hear new funny jokes, you can write them in your journal as well.

I love writing jokes in my journal, because I'm able to look back on not just moments in my life, but also just funny jokes, riddles, and general riffs and banter. Also, if you have a REALLY funny joke, this allows you to never forget it.

59

Seasons And Holidays

Write about the holiday you are experiencing or the season we are in.

What season are we in? Is it Summer, Winter, Autumn, Spring? Are you celebrating a special holiday today?

This journal entry should be written only on holidays that mean a lot to you, or seasons you like the best. What is so good about the holiday or season you are experiencing?

Your favorite seasons and holidays can and will change over time, and it's nice to look back on what you found and find nice or interesting about certain times of the year.

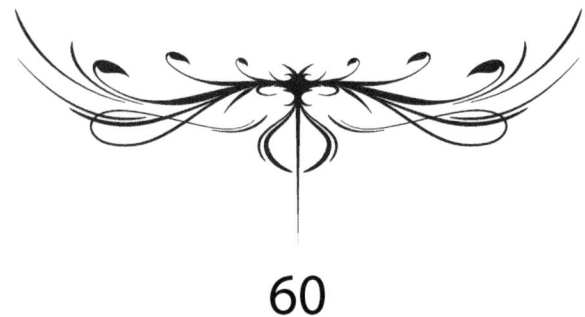

60

Memories

Write about your own memories - ANY memory will do.

I like to call these "flash backs".

Have you ever been just sitting there, and all of a sudden you remember a fond memory that happened months or years ago? THAT right there is a flashback.

It's nice to write about the good memories, but any memory will do for this entry.

Even bad memories are good to look back on and write about. You will learn from these memories. You will pick up on things you previously didn't pick up on. You'll smile, you'll laugh, you may even cry. Get your emotions out on paper, and if you don't want these memories circulating in your physical world, then leave them on paper! - You still get the same emotions out, and they don't need to affect others unless you want them to.

61

Got Problems?

Write down your problems as if you are talking to a therapist.

"Lie down, tell me what's on your mind. Tell me how you FEEL."

Ever hear that before? Maybe not if you've never been to a therapist, psychologist, psychiatrist - but for me, that's the basic word structure - 'tell me how you feel'.

Well, the truth is... you don't need a therapist. As you've probably already found from the other journal templates and entries from this book, just thinking and then writing how you feel and what you experience can bring out the emotions without ever having to tell another soul.

Go ahead - tell your journal what's on your mind. Write about your problems, your set backs, tell your journal how you feel. You'll feel great after, just knowing that you got the energy out, and you can then move on with your life, and don't have to allow your feelings to ever hold you back. You can also learn a heck of a lot from writing as if you are talking to a therapist - in fact, you can be your OWN therapist.

62

Pen Pal

Write to a pen pal, could even be fictional.

Have you ever had a pen pal? I have - and it was one of the coolest things in my childhood.

You know, I forget exactly where my first pen pal was located, or how exactly I got matched up with this pen pal, but it was through my elementary school - all the kids did it.

Usually, pen pals are from a different country - And if not from a different country, they usually have and live a different lifestyle than you.

So, don't just write a letter to a friend - write a letter to someone who is completely different than you. Write about what it's like to celebrate Christmas, because many do not. Write about what it's like to live in a free country, because again... many do not.

Just think about all the things that you do every day, and how and where you live, and then think of the complete opposite. THAT is who you are talking to in this letter.

QUICK TIP: If you don't know "who" (fictionally) you are writing to, just pin point the EXACT opposite side of the globe. Do some quick 5 minute research on who lives in that area of the world, find out the differences between them and you, and then write to them.

63

One Thing

Write about 1 thing you want others to know about.

Think about this one for a minute.

Has there ever been a time where you wanted to tell someone something so badly, but you just couldn't? Maybe they weren't around, maybe no one was around. Maybe that person didn't want to hear it, maybe they were in a bad mood.

Well, now is the time where you are able to tell that one thing you want everyone to know about.

Is there something big happening in your life? Did something good just happen that you are excited about, that you just can't wait to say out loud? Write it down!

On the other side of this journal post, you can also write about something that might not be so happy and exciting. Maybe a pet passed on, maybe you just got some bad news. Even if what just happened is more negative than positive, it is equally important to write about it.

Get out your emotions, learn from them, and by writing these things down, you are able to grow - you, your writing, your future thoughts and feelings and actions, it can all start to change by writing about it.

64

You Don't Even Know Me!

Write about yourself, and think to yourself, "You don't even know me!"

This should be one of the easiest journal entries you ever write.

Have you ever met someone who just didn't understand you, and probably never will? This happens to me almost every day.

But the fact of the matter is, everyone is different. Every single person in this world sees the world we all live in different. Just because we all live on the same planet doesn't mean we all think or act the same.

So, write down a time where someone just didn't understand you, and start off your entry with "You don't even know me!". How the journal entry continues and ends is up to you.

65

This Summer

Write about what you are going or want to do this summer.

What's the plan for this coming summer? Do you even have any plans?

It's always nice to be able to look forward to something. It's even better to write it down, otherwise you might not remember it later on.

You can write things you already plan on doing, or you can write things you wish you could do if your means were better.

Dream, dream, dream. If you really want to go to Costa Rica, or Las Vegas, or do a thousand different cool things this summer but just don't think you will be able to, that's okay - write these things down.

You never know. There could come a time in your life when you are able to do whatever you want, whenever you want. When that time comes, you'll have a list of things you are now able to accomplish and experience in the summer days and months.

66

Politics

You can't talk about politics with almost anyone, write about it here!

Ahhh... politics. The one thing you should never talk about at a dinner party.

But seriously, unless you agree 100% on the politics that someone else believes in, there is bound to be all sorts of conflicts.

Both of my parents are democrats and still argue about certain issues. My brother is a Republican and can agree on some issues, but disagrees with most. I on the other hand don't choose any type of party (but I still have my beliefs!).

The point is, it doesn't matter what "party" you claim. Everyone thinks differently, especially when it comes to politics.

Here I want you to write down what you 'think' your political party is. But even more, I want you to write about the specific aspects and beliefs you have about policy in your country. Rant about it, rave about it, just write it down.

67

Hate?

Write about what you dislike, and why.

Hate is a strong word, I know. So if you don't like the word 'hate', talk about your dislikes instead.

These dislikes can be as small as a type of food, or as big as racism.

I don't want you to put all of your energy into this, but I do want you to think about this entry, for just a few minutes.

It's never good to think or talk about what you dislike all the time, but sometimes it's good to get out the negative energy in order to understand what your dislikes are, so your energy can then be directed to more positive things, like what you DO like.

Think about the things in life you dislike, write them down, and move on. Then, only every once in awhile, look back on these to see how your dislikes and likes change over time.

68

Motivation

Motivate yourself. What do you want to do, and why?

Similar to a motivational speaker, today is the day you become a motivational writer.

Have you ever listened to motivational or inspirational audio, video, maybe even read a book or article or story that motivated you?

What you want to accomplish doesn't matter as much as how you are going to motivate yourself to actually get it accomplished. It starts with the thoughts, then the feelings, then the actions which will lead to results.

You can write about multiple things you want to accomplish, but start with one. Start with that one thing you really want to accomplish right now, and write a motivational post telling you exactly what you need to do to get it done, and WHY it's important that you do it.

When you can read your own thoughts and motivation, it can really inspire you to work on what you need to work on. It all starts with a fresh, inspiring and motivational journal entry.

69

Imagination

Use your imagination, and let it run wild in this entry.

Children have the utmost wild imaginations.

If you are a parent, or if you've been around kids for even a short period of time, you'll find that you are in two completely different worlds.

You could be watching your child push a tiny toy car across the rug, and see it as 'playing'. But in the mind of a child, they are racing in the Indy 500!

In this entry, let your imagination run wild. Let it run far, and don't ever stop and say "What am I writing?". It doesn't matter!

You can start with a color in the room you are in. Then change those walls into a background (sunset, forest, beach?). Maybe your furniture starts talking. Maybe you have a dance with a lamp.

Just start writing, and don't stop until you've finished at least one full page of imaginative thinking. And remember, children don't cut their imaginations short, so don't cut yours short either.

70

Colors Of The Sky

There are so many colors in the sky. Describe them here.

If you believe the sky is blue, then you are sadly mistaken.

Look at the 'sky' from space, and it's black. Look at it in most places in the world, and it's a light blueish white. In other areas, it's orange, yellow, red, purple, even green (seriously)!

So what color is the sky that exists above YOU?

Orange glow, light fluffy whiteish blue/blueish white clouds. The violet/magenta subtle colors stream in through the orangey yellows.

Describe the color of the sky as it is now, and describe how it changes throughout the day (if you know or remember).

71

Solve HUGE Problems

Try to solve huge problems that are going on in the world right now.

World hunger, anyone?

How about racism, sexism, world/country policy, homelessness, world hunger, gang violence, etc.

It is very sad sometimes when you really think hard about the many problems that exist in our world today - especially when some of them didn't exist 1000, 100, even 10 years ago!

Do you have a solution?

It doesn't have to be a solution that you write a letter about to your congressman / congresswoman. You don't even have to know an exact perfect solution.

But when you begin to think about the problems in the world, and start to write down how you think they can be solved, it makes your communication more clear and your beliefs more valid and understandable.

72

Find Out More

Write about something you want to know more about, find out more!

"Just Google it." I hear that 3 word sentence almost every day (sometimes it's 2 words - google it).

But really, it just comes down to basic research.

I can 100% guarantee you one thing in life (feel free to call me out on it if the guarantee fails): You as well as every single person in this world will NEVER know everything about everything. There is also no way any of us could know everything about everything.

What we can do though, is find out more about the things that interest us. I like writing, so I constantly research, read, and write so that I can get better and learn new things. I'm not the best writer in the world, and I don't know everything about writing, so I'm always trying to find out more.

Whatever it is you want to learn more about, go research (google it! haha). Then, when you learn something new that you have never learned before, write it down in your journal. You'll most likely remember it for the rest of your life after writing it, and even if you forget about it, you can still come back to it and re-learn it again in the near or far future.

73

Life In Space

Write about what you think life in space would be like.

Do you ever think about life in space? Life outside of 'the world' we live in (Earth)?

Now, if you are an astronaut or cosmonaut, then you can actually write about your experience in space.

But of course, if you are like the rest of us, and have never been outside of our planet, then you will only have conceptions about how it 'might' be like in space.

Write about it. Is it cold? How do the stars look? What would you do on a foreign planet after landing? Is there gravity, how much? Would you bounce around all day? How would the vehicles look?

Think even further into this topic. I mean, are there moutains and rivers and oceans on other planets? Sure there are, we live in space, an unlimited universe. Everything is everywhere (now think about THAT!).

74

Worst Meal

I've had lots of 'worst' meals. What's your worst meal ever, and why?

Yep, I've had a lot of "worst" meals too.

Sometimes it's what my mom or dad cooked, most of the time it was from a lousy restaurant (and even sometimes good restaurants!).

Don't just write down the name of the meal or dish or food that you didn't like. On top of that, write a detailed description of the meal.

Use descriptive words to explain the meal - sloppy, grimy, wet, cold. Talk about the taste - disgusting, fishy, spicy, bland, woody (ever have chicken that tastes like wood? ;).

Write about why you will never eat this meal again, and why you'll never make it for your own friends, family, kids.

75

Worldly Impact

Write about the impact you can have and want to have on the world.

This journal entry is here to make you think bigger about yourself.

Did you know that you have the power to change the world? Everyone does. I've seen former drug addicts, homeless people, and men and women with literally no money or authority change the world.

The only way this can be made possible is by beginning to think about yourself in a different way.

I don't want you to think of yourself as any sort of 'guru' or 'all knowing entity'. Instead, write down what you are good at, how you think, how you can make someone's life better.

Start small, then work your way bigger and move outward. Do you make music? That can have an impact on the world. Do you have a skill that others don't? That can also have an impact on the world.

Just write about the things you are good at, how they can further impact the world, and how you can get your message heard.

76

Growing Apart

Write about how or why you and your old friend grew apart.

I've had lots of friends, and lots of best friends in my life.

However, I've also grown apart from most of my friends. Especially friends from grade school / elementary school - I don't talk or communicate with any of them any more.

Why did we grow apart? Why don't I talk to them anymore?

This entry shouldn't influence you to call anyone up or anything like that. You grew apart for a reason. Write down that reason. Was it because of you, them - was it mutual? Was it because you went to separate high schools or colleges later in life?

Again, it's not about trying to reconnect with old friends. This entry is more about realizing why we as people grow apart. You are reading this book for a reason, you are sitting or standing where you are right now for a reason. It's the experiences and actions that we've taken that have gotten us to where we are. If you hadn't grown apart from that friend, things in your life may have turned out different. Think about that, and write about what you think about it.

77

Jealousy

Who or what are you jealous of and why? Write about it.

Most people say jealousy is never a good attribute to have. However, jealousy exists in every single one of us, even me.

Now, jealousy isn't the same as expressing jealousy. What I'm saying is, it's okay to be jealous, because that means you are striving to be a greater version of yourself.

I'm jealous of other great writers, but I don't complain about it or express my jealousy towards them. Instead, I think about (and sometimes write about) what or who I am jealous of and why. It allows me to strive to be better.

Write about your jealousy. Then write about what you can do to be better. Before you know it, you'll work so much and so hard that you won't be jealous of that thing or person you were jealous of before.

78

Radio Show

Write about what you would say on your own radio show.

"You are now listening to THE BELL, with Norman T. Bell!"

Start your radio show journal entry with a big, loud intro. From there, it's all up to you on how your radio show sounds and works.

You can write an entire script for what you would actually say on the radio, or you can simply describe how your radio show would sounds, and what sorts of aspects would be a part of it.

Would it be a pure talk show? Would you play music? Would you mix and scratch music and sounds together?

Even think about the callers you would get. What topics would you talk about with them? Would you be a rude talk show host, or an inspirational one?

This entry should be fun, and will simply show you how your own radio show would sound on air.

79

Inventions

Invent your own product, and write about it in a journal entry.

Have you ever thought about a product or invention idea, and then months, weeks, or even days later you find out someone else implemented the idea and made a million bucks from it? Yes, we all have.

So what invention ideas do you have?

It could be one of those "As Seen On TV" deals. It could be a product that you sell in stores. It could even be a digital or information product or service.

Whatever your brain pumps out, just write it down - even if your idea doesn't seem doable. You can always expand on your ideas and even combine ideas together.

Besides making a brand new product, you can also write down your modifications to existing products that would make them better.

And please, if you think of a brand new idea that would add value to people's lives, MAKE IT HAPPEN! Find out how to make your invention a reality, and you too could be one of those people that made millions from a simple idea.

80

Inanimate Object

Write from the point of view of an inanimate object.

I love this journal entry, and I hope you do too.

Think about all the objects, all the 'things' in your life that aren't really alive.

Couches, other furniture, your house, a rug, a toilet, your cell phone - it could be anything.

How does your couch feel after you sit on it's face all day long? Does your keyboard hate you because you continue tapping it's keys? What would a toilet tell you? "Flush twice please!" maybe?

This entry can be very fun, and should be. Pretend you are having a conversation with an inanimate object. Pretend that everything in the entire world came to life, and now you have to hear about it.

I just thought of another one - your toothbrush! How does your toothbrush feel when you use it's hair to wipe away all the gunk and crud from your mouth? Write about it in this entry, and have some fun with it.

81

Country Description

Describe the country you are from or that you live, the good and bad.

What country do you live in? How is it different than other countries? What is good and/or bad about it? What could you do to make it better? What could the leaders in your country do to make it better.

Although this could change in the future, right now I believe that no one country is perfect or ever will be or can be perfect.

There will always be very good things about your country, as well as very bad things.

Maybe your country has certain rights (or lack of rights) that might not be beneficial to you. There are probably laws in place that discriminate against you.

First, write about the good and bad aspects of your country. Then, write about what you can physically do to make your country better. Finally, write the things that your country's leader(s) can do to make your country better.

Even though there might be negative aspects revolving your country, try to keep this entry positive, and focus on solutions to the problems that your country may possess.

82

World Treasures

Write about what you treasure most in the world.

Have you ever been asked this question before? - What do you treasure most in the world?

I remember my former girl friend asked me this question, and trying to be cute, I responded "You, baby". She didn't take it the way I meant it, and claimed I was objectifying her.

Well, my girlfriend won't be reading my journal or yours, so if you treasure your woman or man most in the world, write about it!

But really, what do you treasure most? What couldn't you live without?

This should obviously be something that you own, or something that exists in your life right now. You can save your "wishes and dreams" for other journal entries.

Besides writing about what you treasure most in the world, write about why you treasure it most. Think about why exactly you love this item/object/person so much, and why you just can't continue without it/them.

Then, try this entry a few more times in the near future (maybe over the next year or so), and you'll find that what you treasure most will change as your subconscious mind changes.

83

Else To Do

Write down the to-do list of someone else's daily life.

"Else to do" can also be explained as someone else's to-do list.

Put simply, instead of writing down your own to-do list, write down someone else's to-do list.

This journal entry can do a few things for you.

Most of us believe that we have the biggest to-do list. We think that we have it the hardest, that we have to do more things than other people.

But do we really?

Even though I know in my mind that I may have to write a few thousand words, edit things, proofread books and articles, do speaking engagements, talk with my inner circle on the phone, eat, shower, go to the bank, go to the store, cook dinner - I also know that other people probably have a much longer or even more involved to-do list.

When I begin to write down someone else's to-do list, I find out that other people could very well have more things to do during the day than I do. This allows me to re-think my own to-do list and my own strategy. It also allows me to focus on only the important things I have on my list.

This list doesn't have to be exact, in fact most of it is fictional, and will be more of what you 'think' others have to do. Write about the president's to-do list, or even your family member or friend. Maybe it's a music artist or celebrity you like. Write it down, and think about what more YOU can add to your to-do list, as well as what to cross off.

84

Don't Need

Write about things you have bought but don't really use or need.

For me, this entry has always been very beneficial to me - to the 100th degree in fact!

If you are reading this book, then you have the money and/or resources that others don't have. You probably have a computer or some sort of digital reading device. If this is true, there are probably hundreds of other "things" you have, objects.

Sure, there are things that you 'need', but everyone's 'needs' are different. You don't really need a toothbrush, but many would disagree (I would too, I need my toothbrush).

But what are things in your life that you really don't need? Do you have too many shoes? Maybe you have a basement full of knickknacks, or too many Halloween decorations. Maybe it's something entirely different than any of those.

Whatever it is that comes to mind, write it down. Then, think about selling some of it, giving other stuff away, some you might want to just trash. Look back on this post in the future, and find out what you still have, what you don't, what you use and don't use, and you can re-evaluate what you really, really don't need.

85

Addictions

Write about addictions, whether or not you've been addicted before.

I can admit, I used to be addicted to cigarettes. Some are addicted to food. Others are addicted to much more detrimental things, like hard drugs or physically harming themselves.

Your addictions don't need to be deadly, in fact we all have many tiny addictions. A specific food, brand, even a person.

Write your addictions in this entry, and think about which ones you should work on, and which ones are okay (like being addicted to a spouse or being addicted to healthy food).

Then, pick one addiction in your 'to work on' list, and work on it! Try to cut down on this one addiction. Your willpower will increase, you'll start to cut down on other bad addictions, and when you come back to this journal entry later on, you can X out other addictions you've gotten rid of.

86

Difficult Convos

Write about a difficult conversation you've had with another person.

Have you ever had one of those conversations? You know, the ones where your heart is at your feet, your mouth gets dry, your swallowing and sweating like crazy?

We've all had a conversation like that in our life (probably many). Whether or not you've kept that emotion inside you, it's time to get it out on paper.

Write about how you felt in a specific conversation you had with someone. What did they say? Why did it make you feel the way you did? Could you have done anything different to have made the conversation easier?

The more you think about this and just get it out on paper, the quicker you can move on from it and continue on with your life. You don't have to keep this on your shoulders forever. Get it out, get rid of the feeling, and move on to the better conversations you will have in the future.

87

Lost Everything

What if you lost everything today? Write about what you would do.

You've heard it all over the place. The news, media, online. People are losing everything in crime, natural disasters, and other devastation that has taken literally everything from them.

If you've already lost everything before, write about it. If you haven't, think about how you would feel if you did.

How would you start over from scratch? What would you do first? Would you try to rebuild your life where it is, or move somewhere new?

There are many questions you can ask yourself about losing your life, your home, your belongings. Make a plan if you want, even if it's the first few steps. It's always best to be prepared, and to think about not only how you will handle it, but also how others who have lost everything feel.

88

Regret

Have any regrets? Write about things you regret saying or doing.

We all have regrets in life.

Things you've said, things you've done, even things you haven't said or done.

Whatever you regret in your life, write it down. For you, it might be hard to think of a regret, but think a little longer and you'll find one in your subconscious memory. At first thought, I'm not able to think of any regrets. But after a minute or two, I'll have a list of 5 or 10.

This is again one of those things you shouldn't dedicate all of your energy to, or think about for a long time. Instead, think about and write about your regrets to make sure you don't make the same types of decisions that you would regret in the future.

89

One Year

What would you do if you had one year exactly to live?

One year left, what would you do? This entry has a simple concept, but you can make it as complex as you want.

Also, think about what you would do depending on whether or not everyone else in the world had a year left to live as well. Those two experiences would be very different (think about it).

Describe the things you would do, the places you would go, the people you would meet. Make sure all of these things can fit in one year.

Once you are done with your list, make a plan to do them before you aren't able to anymore. You just listed all the things you could physically do in one year. Well, about how many years do you have left in your life? If it's more than one year, it's more time than you need to accomplish them.

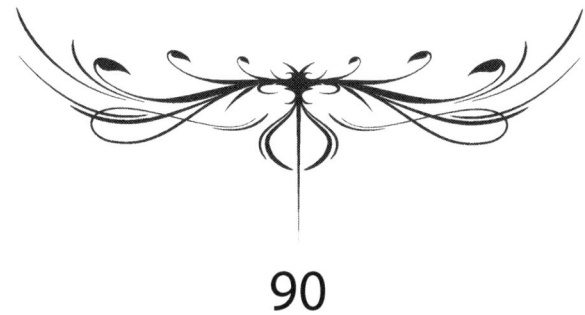

90

Lyric Dissection

Dissect the lyrics of your favorite song(s). Find their true meaning.

You'd be surprised how different the lyrics are than the way the songs sound.

I hear 6 year old girls rapping and singing about sex, violence, misogyny. I hear young boys rapping and singing about the same things.

It doesn't really matter what age you are though, most people don't really understand the lyrics that they sing and dance along to.

Think of your favorite song. Listen to it, sing it, dance to it, bob your head to it. Then search the lyrics. Now listen to the song again, but read each word as the song goes on. Different, huh? Starting to notice things?

You can take it a step further (for most songs anyway) and search for and find out the meaning of the lyrics. This is where you might say "Woah, I had no idea..."

This can be funny, enjoyable, or even a bit mind blowing. You can choose to write the lyrics, or what they mean, or both.

91

Traditions

Write about the various traditions you follow, and why you follow them.

When you think about it, you have adapted to certain traditions in your life.

These traditions can be core traditions that you adopt from your parent(s)/guardian(s) as soon as you are born, or even little traditions like Wednesday night tacos, or monthly bike rides, or yearly summer camping trips.

Write down all the traditions you follow that you can think of, but more importantly why you follow them. Have you followed them your entire life? Was it someone else who taught you the tradition? Did the tradition come about organically and naturally (it's just something you 'do')?

This should be interesting to see how you started a tradition, why you still follow it, and you might even find out about traditions that you didn't know you followed.

92

Wonder

What sorts of things do you really wonder about in the world?

What do you wonder about? Take caution, this could really make you think for awhile.

You can make this as simple or as complex as you want. Do you think about random things like how your fingernails grow or why certain people grow more hair than others?

Or do you wonder about bigger things, like how the world really started, or what sorts of planets exist in other galaxies, and what life forms exist out there?

Either way, it's always good to wonder - it's what makes this world wonderful. It's always fun to do this journal entry again in the future, as you can start to make a list and wonder even more (as well as wonder less, and get more clear).

93

Happiness

Write about what makes you truly 100% happy.

You may be more happy than others, you may be more sad than others. All of us are happy or have been happy at least one time in our lives.

What makes you truly happy? What is the one thing that puts a smile on your face, and keeps it there?

This could be going on vacation, it could be a person in your life, it could even be a special meal or moment.

Write about why this thing/event/experience/person makes you happy. What is it exactly that makes you happy, that makes you smile, that puts you in a place of ease and freedom?

When you write about positive emotions like happiness, it can help you be more happy in the present and future, and will remind you of the feeling you have when you are happy, and what you should do to make you happy.

94

Backwards

Write this entire journal entry backwards!

This journal entry is fun, but can be a little difficult. Once you are finished, it might even be hilarious to read it.

There are two ways you can do this. The first is starting at the bottom of the page, and write your entry backwards word by word. The second is starting at the bottom of the page, but writing your entry letter by letter. You can also choose to do both.

Write about whatever you want. Choose one of the many journal entry ideas, make your own, or just freewrite.

Once you are done, try reading your article backwards (how you wrote it), and see if you can read it backwards as skillfully as you can if it were forwards.

Then, read it from top to bottom, and see if any of it makes sense, or if you can even read it properly. There may even be a hidden message or two in your backwards writing.

95

Perspective

Write about your differing perspective from other people.

What's your perspective on [insert topic or situation here]?

We all have different perspectives - even if that means your perspective is not having a perspective.

Think of one or more ideas or thoughts you have that others don't agree on. Write these topics or situations in your journal.

Then, write about why you think the other person/people disagreed with you. Finally, think about these situations in the perspective of others. Write down how you think other people would think about a topic.

You can either learn a lot from this entry, and/or expand on your own perspectives (and quite possibly change them).

96

Buzzing About

What are people buzzing about, and why?

Social media, news, friends, family, TV, newspapers, radio - you hear from at least one of those each day.

So, what are people buzzing about?

Is everyone mad about money? Are people crazy over a recent celebrity mishap? Did a new gadget get released in the past week?

You can choose to write a list of everything that people have been talking about, or write about one specific buzzing topic in more detail.

Write about why you think this topic became so popular, and when you think it will fade. Has there ever been any popular media you missed out on completely?

Sometimes you will learn more about important topics, and other times you'll laugh at the fact that people even found a certain topic interesting or valuable.

97

Taste Description

Describe things with taste - things that you wouldn't normally eat.

As a child, you probably tasted everything you could get your hands on. I remember getting my teeth on furniture, toys, plastic, wood, and many other items as a kid.

I'm not asking you to taste inedible objects around you. But what if you did? THAT is what you will write about. If you took a bite out of a tennis ball, how would it taste? Furry? Salty? Dirty? Once you get to the inside, it might taste rubbery.

This journal entry uses your taste sense and your brain, and expands your thinking on how things taste, as well as develops creative new words for how things taste.

98

Thesaurus Your Way

Describe something, anything, then thesaurus your way to new words.

This journal writing template is easy to do, but it is also very beneficial - Not only to your writing, but also to your general grammar and IQ.

Start with any word or thing. Me. My sister. Piano. Sky. River.

Then, start to describe it. For river: flowing, blue, white, rushing, extravagant. Then pick one of your descriptive adjectives, and expand on it.

Some words will be more difficult to find synonyms than others. So, take out a thesaurus, or use the online thesaurus.

Write down all of the synonyms for your descriptive word. You can even circle the words that actually make sense with what you are describing. This will get you to learn new words, and will enhance your grammar and basic coversation and public speaking.

99

Advice

If you could give advice to someone you know (or don't know), what advice would you give them?

This should be the easiest journal entry you ever write.

Whether we speak it out loud or keep it to ourselves, we all have advice for someone else (usually everyone). Not everyone likes advice, so most of the time our advice stays in our head.

It's time to put that advice on paper. Pick someone who you believe you can help, and write down the advice you would give them. You can write about a personal friend or family member, a celebrity or someone famous, or any other real or fictional person.

Come back to this journal entry some time from now, and you will find that some of your advice was beneficial, while some other advice wouldn't have helped at all. If you find advice that you think was actually the wrong advice, that's good, because it means you as a person are growing.

Thanks For Reading!

Thanks you so much for reading!

I really hope you enjoyed these 99 journal writing templates and prompts. As you can see, you can open up a whole new world of journaling and writing in general when you apply just a few of these templates in your personal AND public writing.

You can really learn a lot about yourself, others, and the world - just by writing a new journal entry every day.

Have you ever regretted not being able to remember everything in your past? I know I do... That's why I started journaling, so I can remember the good, the ugly, and everything in between.

Journaling allows me to figure out new ideas that I wouldn't have figured out or even ventured into without journal writing.

Now before you go outside or go hang out with friends, make sure you write a journal entry, even if it is small. Just pick your favorite journal prompt and RUN WITH IT.

Again, I hope you enjoyed the book and the journal writing templates and prompts, thanks for reading.